# RE-TREAT YOUR FAMILY TO LENT

Sandra DeGidio, O.S.M.

*Nihil Obstat:*
    Rev. Hilarion Kistner, O.F.M.
    Rev. John J. Jennings

*Imprimi Potest:*
    Rev. Jeremy Harrington, O.F.M.
    Provincial

*Imprimatur:*
    Rev. John L. Cavanaugh, V.G.
    Archdiocese of Cincinnati
    February 11, 1983

The *Nihil Obstat* and *Imprimatur* are a declaration that a book or pamphlet is considered to be free from doctrinal or moral error. It is not implied that those who have granted the *Nihil Obstat* and *Imprimatur* agree with the contents, opinions or statements expressed.

Cover and book design by Julie Lonneman.

SBN 0-86716-022-5

© 1983, Sandra DeGidio
St. Anthony Messenger Press
All rights reserved.
Printed in the U.S.A.

# Foreword

Twelve years ago, when I first started working with families, one of the most repeated requests from parents was: "Give us some ideas for ways that our family can observe and celebrate Lent together." So with trusty typewriter and magic Xerox machine, I put together a little booklet of ideas for families to use at home each year during Lent.

Three years ago I left parish family ministry to minister to families as a free-lance writer and lecturer. In those three years, one of the most repeated requests I heard from the parents in the parish that I left was: "Why don't you publish those Lenten family ideas you gave us? Our Xeroxed copies are falling apart."

So, for all those families with tattered copies and for the thousands of parents I've met around the country who have made the same sort of request, I offer this little book. I offer it as gift. May it become totally gift as it is shared by each of you. In that sharing, may you reveal your own precious giftedness to one another and bring to each other the promise and the reality of new life.

# Contents

Introduction  1

Shrove Tuesday/Ash Wednesday: Beginning Lent  5
      6   Family Fat Tuesday Celebration
      6   Family Ash Wednesday Celebration

The First Full Week of Lent: Prayer  9
    12   Family Prayer Corner
    12   Morning and Evening Prayer for Lent

The Second Week of Lent: Fasting  15
    18   Family Fasting Activity

The Third Week of Lent: Baptism  21
    24   Family Baptism Remembrance

The Fourth Week of Lent: Almsgiving  27
    31   Family Almsgiving Activity

The Fifth Week of Lent: Springtime  33
    36   Family Springtime/New Life Activity

The Climax of Lent: Holy Week  39
    40   Passion Sunday
    41   Holy Thursday
    42   Good Friday
    42   The Easter Vigil
    44   Easter Sunday

Beyond Lent: The Easter Season  49

# Introduction

Most of us remember Lents when we gave up candy and movies and watched our parents make heroic efforts to stop smoking. Rising early for daily Mass was often part of the season. We heard about fast and abstinence and, as we grew up, experienced them (along, too often, with various techniques for getting around them). Purple vestments, Stations of the Cross, and purple covers on statues and crosses the last week were all part of former Lents. Let's really be nostalgic: Do you remember the lace and satin repository of Holy Thursday, the wooden clapper and silenced organ of Good Friday?

Quietly, almost without our noticing, many of those external observations disappeared. But we still have Lent. We still have these six weeks of March and early April when the brown, weary dreariness of winter slowly gives way to the new life and light of spring.

We would do well to allow that natural change of seasons to speak to us. The struggle between warmth and cold, the great desire we have at this time of year to see something green and flowering break through the gray snow and brown mud—all of these very natural occurrences speak to us of our need for renewal, for change. It is no accident that the Church in her wisdom gives us the season of Lent at this time of year. Lent is a time of concentrated effort toward rebirth, a time to get back to the basics of Christian living. It is a time of renewal and reconciliation, of penance and prayer, of fasting and almsgiving.

In the rhythm of family life, there is periodic need for the renewal that is Lent. We can get so caught up in "business-as-usual" that we fail to notice how we may have grown away from one another and consequently away from God. Lent is a time to reverse that separation.

Lent is a time of *retreat* in the real sense of that term: a time of turning back, of turning away from that which is dangerous to our spiritual growth, a time of re-turning to the Lord. Lent is a time for the entire family to make a concentrated effort to be more attentive to one another and to the Lord. It is a time to re-treat ourselves to the good in God and in one another; a time to re-treat ourselves to the new life that can be ours.

The perennial problem in families, however, seems to be: How can our children best understand the 40 days of Lent? How can they learn the real meaning of renewal and reconciliation, penance and prayer, fasting and almsgiving? The answer, of course is by experiencing them within the family. Children learn the abstract realities of renewal and reconciliation by the way their parents live those realities. And Lent is a perfect time to show our children how to live those aspects of Christianity.

But before we can demonstrate to our children what Lent is about, we have to know what it means to us. It does no good to encourage our children to fast, pray or share if they do not see us living what we say. A family is only as spiritually healthy as the parents of the family. Therefore, each chapter of this book will begin with some thoughts for parents on an aspect of Lent (beginning Lent, prayer, fasting, Baptism, almsgiving, new life, Holy Week), and then suggest a related family experience or activity.

Forty days is a long time for children. It is important that, in our good intentions to celebrate Lent with intensity and determination, we do not make commitments for ourselves and our families which are bigger than we can reasonably handle. In this book I suggest one activity for each week which you may wish to attempt with your family. It is possible that you may carry some of the activities into successive weeks, but this is not necessarily the intent of the approach. I encourage you to concentrate on only one aspect of Lent each week, rather than committing yourselves to one or more actions for the whole of Lent.

Children learn best by doing. Lent is prime time for doing things which bring us closer to one another and to the Lord. Children are natural tradition-makers. Dolores Curran says that "once is a tradition for children," and she is right. You may find that some of the activities suggested in this book will become family traditions. All of the suggestions have been used successfully by families; many are family traditions for them. They are offered to you in the hope that your family will experience a growth in faith together during this season, and that your family celebrations for Lent and Easter will indeed re-turn and re-treat you to one another and to the Lord.

## Shrove Tuesday/Ash Wednesday:
# Beginning Lent

Special seasons need special beginnings. The dramatic beginning of Lent, Ash Wednesday, is further highlighted by the celebration the day before of Shrove Tuesday, affectionately referred to as "Fat Tuesday" (Mardi Gras).

Gabe Huck points out in his *Book of Family Prayer* that, historically, "when people's lives were dictated by the climate, the end of winter meant a scarcity of provisions. And what meat, frozen or salted, remained was in danger of spoiling with the occasional warm days. Rather than that, people held festivals to consume at one happy time all that was left of the meat. Our word *carnival* originally applied to this end-of-winter holiday; it means 'good-bye to the meat.'" Mardi Gras, "Fat Tuesday," is such a festival.

But with the meat gone and the party over, some weeks of low rations confronted our ancestors. And so, in the centuries when our faith was spreading across Europe, the natural penance of springtime became the Lent of the Church. The day after the party became a second, more somber celebration which we have come to call Ash Wednesday.

Lent became for the early Christians a time of renewal, of return to the Lord. Once a year, in the season when life and death were struggling for control of the earth, Christians struggled with the evil within them and around them.

As a family, begin Lent in the spirit of our early ancestors by celebrating both Fat Tuesday and Ash Wednesday.

### Family Fat Tuesday Celebration

On the Tuesday before Ash Wednesday, have a special family Mardi Gras or Fat Tuesday celebration. Splurge a little! Have the family's favorite meat (and don't serve it again until Lent is over). Have a special dessert. During the meal tell children the story of the origin of Fat Tuesday. Play some games, pop some corn, make banana splits—whatever your family likes to do on special occasions. But remember, all the food that is prepared must be consumed—no leftovers allowed. As bedtime approaches, call for absolute silence while all help with the cleanup. The beginning of Lent is just a few hours away.

### Family Ash Wednesday Celebration

Ash Wednesday is the complete opposite of Fat Tuesday. The mood is quiet, the food is sparse. After the evening meatless meal (Ash Wednesday is a day of abstinence), gather the family together. An older child or parent reads the following from the prophet Joel:

> "But now, now— it is Yahweh who speaks—
> Come back to me with all your heart,...
> turn to Yahweh your God again,
> for he is all tenderness and compassion,
> slow to anger, rich in graciousness,

and ready to relent."
<br>(Joel 2:12-13, *Jerusalem Bible*)

Allow a few minutes for thought during which each member of the family decides which personal faults he or she detests most. These are written on small pieces of paper, crumpled and placed in a brazier to be burned with last year's palm. You might want to cut a wisp of hair from each person's head to be burned also. Light the fire and watch as a part of you is turned quickly to ashes. As the fire burns, the parent says: "Lord have mercy on us, forgive us, and help us to do better in the future." Then stand in silence until the flame dies out.

While the contents of the brazier are cooling, the family might discuss the meaning of Lent and what each person or the household as a whole is going to do to grow during the rest of the week.

When the ashes are cool, the oldest person in the family takes them and marks the forehead of the next oldest saying, "Begin Lent and return to the Lord," and so through the entire family until the youngest marks the oldest. The service can be concluded with a song or you might pray the Lord's Prayer together.

This service can be used at home even if the family participates in the Ash Wednesday service at the parish. Children love repetition, and the service at the parish may become more meaningful to them if they pray a similar service at home.

# The First Full Week of Lent:
# Prayer

Prayer is integral to Lent. But I have a suspicion that most of us have a rather narrow concept of prayer and, consequently, often find ourselves discouraged with our attempts at personal and/or family prayer.

For many of us who grew up in Catholic families, prayer means saying certain words at certain times. We learned the words as children; we also learned to categorize our life into sacred and secular moments. Thus we have prayer times and other times. But prayer is not an isolated activity or a structured formula. It is not just a skill to be mastered or a subject to be studied. Prayer is a way of life.

Prayer is a stance we take toward God and life. It is an expression of our relationship with God and the world around us. Prayer might be praying the rosary or the Stations of the Cross, or it might be quiet meditation, or it might be focusing on one word from a Scripture reading. But it might also be appreciating a work of art; watching a sunrise; feeding wild birds in winter; allowing a film, novel or piece of poetry to touch us deeply. It might be as simple as enjoying our children at play, showing our love to our spouse or being awed by the magnificence of a mountain or an ocean.

We need to see all of life as prayer. We can do this by intensifying every moment, by allowing life situations to speak to us, by responding radically to even the most mundane situations. Then prayer will be as much a part of our lives as breathing, and the dictum "pray always" (see Ephesians 6:18, 1 Thessalonians 5:17) will be a reality in our lives.

As the author James Carroll puts it: "Prayer is tending *toward* the presence of God....To pray is to listen, to tune in, to pay attention to the prayer of the Spirit within us. Thus prayer, in this sense, is not so much something we do as it is a way of seeing and hearing what is in fact *already* being done" (*Prayer From Where We Are).*

The Gospel for the first Sunday of Lent tells us that Jesus went to the desert where he prayed and fasted for 40 days. Prayer is the heart of fasting and almsgiving. It is the heart of everything we do. It calls our actions into existence and gives them life. We live our prayer, whether we want to admit it or not. Our prayer life is expressed in all we do, and what we do affects those around us and says a great deal about who we are.

There are times when, like Jesus, we need to go away into the desert—into a quiet, desolate place—to investigate the state of our prayer by looking seriously and honestly at the state of our life. Lent is one of those times.

And so I invite you to go to wherever your desert is and reflect on some questions about prayer. Then decide what you will do for yourself this Lent to return to the Lord in prayer, to re-treat yourself to renewed prayerfulness.

What you do will have more effect on your children than you know. Children are great observers and imitators. They learn to pray by watching how you pray and by praying with you. Children are not made prayerful by learning prayers and being reminded to say them, but by living and praying with prayerful parents. Ask yourself:

- Do I live at such a rapid pace that I have no time for reflection on what is happening in my life? No time for stillness? No time to search for the inner meaning of events and persons in my life?
- How can prayer become a power in my life that enables me to meet life's demands, challenges and beauties?
- What needs to change in my life-style so that I can "pray always"?
- Is my concept of prayer so limited to time, space or a specific formula that I am not open to new experiences of prayer?
- As a parent, do I pray *with* my children? Are there ways I can help my family grow in prayer? Do my children ever see me pray apart from mealtime or bedtime?
- Have I ever taken time to think about who God is for me? What is my relationship with God? Has it changed over the years?
- Where in my life do I need to be reconciled with myself? With the Lord? With other people? What can I do to help that reconciliation process?
- Have I taught my children prayers, or do I teach them to pray?
- Can I spend some time each week reflecting on the Scriptures?
- Are there ways I can enter more fully into the prayer of the parish at Sunday Mass—such as reflecting on the readings, participating more in singing, getting to Mass on time, listening more

carefully to the words we pray together?

This week's family experience is two-pronged. You may want to try both activities or just one of them. Or you may want to continue your own family Lenten prayer traditions.

### Family Prayer Corner

In the spirit of Jesus' trip to the desert for prayer and reflection, develop a "desert place" in your home. Let this be a total family endeavor.

Gather the family together to decide on a place in the house that can be designated a prayer corner. Choose a place where the family or individuals can go to pray, think or read and be assured of quiet and privacy. (One family that I know chose a corner in the parents' bedroom.) Put a small table in the corner. Enthrone a Bible (a children's Bible, too) on a purple or white cloth. Add a candle, a cross and a cactus, if you have one, to give the idea of a desert place. Family members can add to the prayer corner whatever makes the space more conducive to prayerfulness for them. The important thing is that it remain a place set apart for prayer and quiet. Family members using the prayer corner may not be disturbed, not even by phone calls!

Perhaps a family resolution for the week could be that each member of the family spend at least 10 minutes a day alone in the prayer corner.

The prayer corner may also be used for praying together as a family.

### Morning and Evening Prayer for Lent

If you already have a traditional family Lenten prayer, I encourage you to continue it. The following is a suggestion for family morning and evening prayer you might like to try this week:

A common prayer/penance of Lent past was to rise very early for daily Mass. Try gathering the whole family together each morning this week before everyone leaves for the day. Facing east, all take a deep breath, then pray together with gestures:

*With arms at your sides:* Glory to the Father!
*With arms raised in front of you:* Glory to the Son!
*With arms raised above the head:* Glory to the Spirit!
*Lowering arms slowly:* May God watch over each of us and bless us today.

Let a different family member lead this prayer each day. One day get up early enough to greet the sunrise with your morning prayer.

In the evening, before everyone retires or leaves for evening activities, pray the same prayer, this time facing west, with the gestures reversed:

*With arms raised above the head:* Glory to the Father!
*With arms raised in front of you:* Glory to the Son!
*With arms at your side:* Glory to the Spirit! May God watch over each of us and bless us tonight.

# The Second Week of Lent:
# Fasting

Don't you believe that fasting is a good thing! That is *not* a question, it's a statement. Fasting, of itself, is not good. It may punish you, cause your stomach to growl, make you feel penitential, even help you lose weight, but that does not make it good.

I'm glad I said that! I've never liked fasting. I grew up in a family that believed that food on the table five times a day and slightly chunky children were a sign of God's favor. Fasting seemed somehow incompatible with that experience. Yet the year I turned 21 (the legal age for fasting during Lent), my birthday fell on Ash Wednesday! So I fasted. (Except, of course, for the milkshakes between meals—but they were drunk, not eaten.)

Most of us, I would venture, were fairly relieved when the Lenten fasting rules were relaxed. In spite of our relief, I should like to suggest that a recovery of that Lenten discipline can lead to a clearer witness among contemporary Christians to the call of the gospel. Fasting is a gospel value—but not fasting alone: Fasting and almsgiving are gospel twins.

St. Augustine put it well when he said: "Fasting

punishes you, but it will not restore your brother! Your privations will be fruitful if you provide for the needs of another. Certainly you have deprived your body, but to whom did you give that which you deprived yourself? What did you do with the things you denied yourself? How many poor people could be nourished by the meal which you did not take today? Fast, then, in such a way that when another has eaten in your place you may rejoice in the meal you have not taken. Then your offering will be received by God."

For the early Christians, going without meat was "enabling a neighbor to eat." About the year 128 St. Aristides, a philosopher and journalist, explained to the Emperor Hadrian the manner in which Christians lived: "When someone is poor among them, who has need of help, they fast for two or three days, and they have the custom of sending him the food which they had prepared for themselves."

We fast in order to place ourselves in solidarity with the poor. If the grocery money saved by our fasting is not given to the poor, to those who are hungry, then our fasting is empty and useless.

So this year perhaps we could revive the tradition of fasting and aid the world's hungry just a bit. The bishops of the United States have asked that we add one or two fast days a week; maybe we could add one or two abstinence days too. Or perhaps we could eliminate soft drinks or alcoholic beverages during Lent. These, too, are related to world hunger.

Schoolgoers of the family can also return to the Lord through fasting. Ask them to take a look at their lunch at school. Do they take more than they can eat? Do they throw away food they don't want or like? How much wasted food do they see in the lunch room each day? Can they discover reasons for the waste? Could they try to work on the problem with their friends?

Fasting from food and giving of the excess of our lives becomes easier when we reflect on the ancient words of the prophet Isaiah:

> "We have fasted before you," they say. "Why aren't you impressed? Why don't you see our sacrifices? Why don't you hear our prayers? We have done much penance, and you don't even notice it!" I'll tell you why! Because you are living in evil pleasure even while you are fasting, and you keep right on oppressing your workers. Look, what good is fasting when you keep on fighting and quarreling? This kind of fasting will never get you anywhere with me. Is this what I want—this doing of penance and bowing like reeds in the wind and putting on sackcloth and covering yourselves with ashes? Is this what you call fasting?
>
> No, the kind of fast I want is that you stop oppressing those who work for you and treat them fairly and give them what they earn. I want you to share your food with the hungry and bring right into your own homes those who are helpless, poor and destitute. Clothe those who are cold and don't hide from relatives who need your help. If you do these things, God will shed his own glorious light upon you. He will heal you.
> (Isaiah 58:3-8, *The Living Bible*)

Because fasting has long been associated with doing without food, we do not often see it as doing without other things besides food. For example:

- Do without a little sleep; use the time to read or pray.
- Do without anger, impatience, or whatever really

hinders you from returning to the Lord.
- Do without the radio or stereo for a time each day; re-treat yourself and those around you to the joys of a little silence.
- Limit TV to one hour a day.
- Take fewer drugs (from aspirin to alcohol).
- If you are a night owl, go to bed an hour earlier each night (if you can't sleep, use the time for meditation).

Care and effort to be more human can also be a form of fasting. For many of us today, to stop rushing about and jamming our lives with busyness, noisy distraction and anxiety could be a true form of fasting. Such fasting calls us to quiet our lives in order that we might live more deeply and with more meaning. It calls us to care enough to listen and see and feel in a more human way. To be more human we need to attend to human values, as we do when we take time to enjoy neglected family or friends, or to let a family meal express unity and love, or to feel—really feel—the misery of another human being.

These actions mean fasting from the selfishness and status-seeking of our own egos and allowing ourselves to be a bit more vulnerable. They might be more difficult than eating less food, but they are forms of fasting that can re-treat us to Christian love and joy.

### Family Fasting Activity

This week I invite you to set aside at least one half hour during which your family can discuss the concept of fasting and what it means for you. From the examples given above, see if your family can come up with a form of family fast for this week. One family came up with the following:

Each evening an empty place is set at the family

dinner table to remind the family of the hungry. At the end of dinner, the cook tells what is planned for the next day's dinner. Then one of the family (depending on whose turn it is) decides which item on the menu to eliminate. The money that item would cost goes into the plate at the empty place. For example, when spaghetti, salad and garlic bread are on the menu, someone might suggest, "Let's not have meat in the spaghetti sauce." Into the plate goes $3.00.

At the end of the week the money saved is given to those in your community you think need it most. You may have to do some research to determine who that is. To make the project even more immediate to you and your children, you might take the money, go together to the grocery store, buy as many balanced meals as you can with it and bring the food to the local food shelf or to a family who could really use it. Let your children help pick out the foods. You might be surprised at what shopping for food can teach them about healthy eating habits and their own tastes and wastes.

If your family chooses a fasting activity similar to this one, you might want to try the following grace before meals to help emphasize the relationship between your fasting and your almsgiving. Family members can take turns being the leader.

*Leader:* In the name of the Father, and of the Son, and of the Holy Spirit.
  *All:* Amen.
*Leader:* Before sharing this food tonight let us remember that God is here with us. Let us thank him for his goodness to us. (*Family members may mention things for which they are grateful.*)
*Leader:* Lord God of all creation, you made us to care about our many brothers and sisters in this world who are hungry and thirsty, who are in need of

our love and concern. As we share this meal with each other, let us remember those who are hungry tonight.

*Parent:* *(Placing the money not used for food at this meal into the empty plate):* This is the money we would have spent if we had a bigger meal tonight. Bless the little which we are doing, Lord. Bless and multiply it, that it might help in some small way to serve the needs of those who are hungry.

*All:* Amen.

# The Third Week of Lent:
# Baptism

Lent originated because of Baptism. As Christianity spread and adults requested entrance into the community of Christians, the Easter Vigil became the time new converts were initiated. Lent signaled the final stages in their preparation for Baptism.

An Order of Catechumens was established in the Church for those who were preparing to become part of the community. Remember the Mass of the Catechumens (the Liturgy of the Word)? That was the only part of the Eucharistic celebration in which the catechumens could participate. They were asked to leave after the homily, and only those who were already baptized could stay for the Mass of the Faithful (Liturgy of the Eucharist).

As time went on an Order of Penitents was established to allow those who had publicly denied the faith to make amends for their sin and return to the Lord and to the Church. (This developed in response to the sins of apostasy during times of Church persecution.) Thus Lent became a time for penitence as well as for Baptism preparation.

Gradually, adult initiation and the Order of

Catechumens gave way to infant Baptism; and public penance during Lent gave way to a penitential attitude for all. But throughout history these two elements—Baptism and repentance—remained essential to the season.

Today most of us (and our children) were baptized as infants. If you happen to be a convert to Catholicism, your initiation into the Church was probably a pretty private occasion—a few meetings with a priest, a private ceremony one Sunday afternoon in a darkened church with only the closest friends or relatives present.

But during the first 200 years of the Church's history, both baptismal preparation and Baptism itself were public affairs. The entire process took place step by step in the presence of the Christian community. Prospective candidates spent as long as three years readying themselves for Baptism. Lent became a pre-Baptism retreat for them. Those already baptized joined them in this retreat through their own Lenten disciplines so that they, too, could experience a conversion, a return to the Lord. The already baptized prepared to renew their own baptismal vows at the Easter Vigil. They prepared themselves to be a people of faith, worthy to welcome new members into their community.

The catechumens became a reminder to those already baptized of their own baptismal commitment. The community, in addition, was expected to pray for the catechumens, to support them on their journey to Baptism and to witness gospel living for them.

The beginning of Lent found the catechumens standing before the Christian community requesting the sacraments of initiation (Baptism, Confirmation and First Eucharist) and the Christian community affirming God's call to the candidates to be one with them. At the conclusion of Lent, during the Easter Vigil, the sacraments of initiation were celebrated in the presence of that same community.

I relate all of this not just because it is interesting historical background but because in 1972 the renewed *Rite of Christian Initiation of Adults* restored this original procedure to today's Church. Many parishes across the country have begun implementing it. As a result, adult Baptism is no longer a private affair. The presence of adult catechumens in our Church recalls for us the public mission to which Baptism calls each of us.

Lent and Easter are the time when we who were baptized as infants renew our baptismal commitment so that we can be witnesses of gospel living and support those in our community who are preparing for Baptism, whether they are adults or children. Lent is the ideal time to re-treat ourselves to the truth that our lives reflect the depth of our commitment to Jesus, and that our renunciation of evil is a constant struggle.

TV commericals keep trying to convince us that Kodak is America's storyteller. I disagree. I believe that parents, grandparents and families are America's storytellers. The liturgical readings during Lent and Easter are filled with images of water and Baptism. In our history as a people of God, water is a powerful symbol of the life to which the Lord calls us. We hear told and retold the many stories of the importance of water in our lives. We would do well to reread those stories this week, remembering that it is through the symbol of water that we respond to God's call and experience conversion in Baptism:

- Begin with the creation story (see Genesis 1:1-31). God's spirit hovered over the waters, and the waters were filled with new life.
- In the story of Noah (see Genesis 6:13—8:14), God destroyed the torrents of sin with torrents of water and, when the waters subsided, the dove returned with the green branch of new life.

- It was a march through water that brought freedom and new life to Moses and the Israelites (see Exodus 13:17—15:27).
- Jesus was baptized in the waters of the Jordan River (see Matthew 3:13-17) and became for us the fountain of living water that we hear about in the Gospel for the third Sunday of Lent, Cycle A (John 4:5-42). In Baptism we receive this living water and rise to new life in Jesus Christ.

After you have read these Scripture stories, meditate on the meaning of Baptism in your own life: your own plunge into the floodwaters of death and resurrection with Jesus, your own journey to freedom through the cleansing waters of Baptism, your own call from God to a life of discipleship.

Then, each night this week, tell your children one of the stories. Don't make any connections for them, don't add any morals—and don't read them. *Tell* them. In the telling, something of yourself and your faith will be shared that no mere reading could reveal.

Tell them also about the process of initiation that the early Christians experienced. If your parish has catechumens, try to attend the liturgies where they are present. Show your children, through your actions toward those catechumens, what it means to be a living witness of the gospel. Take time after Mass to stop and talk with the catechumens. It is up to you, the already baptized, to make them feel welcome. Add a prayer for those preparing for Baptism to your morning, evening or meal prayers.

## Family Baptism Remembrance

After you have told and lived all of these stories with your children, tell them the story of their own Baptism.

Place a bowl of water on a table in your prayer

corner or in your living or dining area. Resurrect the family photo album. Display photos of everyone's Baptism. Find the white garments, baptismal candles and certificates, and put them out also. Maybe even call or write grandmas and grandpas for photos, certificates or garments of your own.

Gather the family around the artifacts of Baptisms past and tell each child about his or her Baptism: When and where did the Baptism take place? What was the weather like? Who was there? What did you eat? Did the baby cry? Why did you choose these godparents? What were your feelings that day? If your children's sponsors live nearby, invite them to come share in the storytelling. If grandparents live near, invite them to tell the story of *your* Baptism. This week, make your family America's storyteller.

If you like, end the evening by asking everyone to respond as a group to the following questions which attempt to elaborate on the implication of our baptismal promises:

- Do you believe in God, the Creator of all that is good?
- Do you believe that goodness includes even you with all your faults, failings and weaknesses?
- Do you believe that Jesus is brother and Savior?
- Do you believe in joy and humor, creativity and spontaneity even at the risk of being different?
- Do you believe that people who say they love God but dislike their neighbor are liars? (See 1 John 4:20.)
- Do you believe that what you do to someone else you do to Jesus? (See Matthew 25:31-46.)
- Do you renounce the spirit of evil around you?
- Do you renounce the spirit of selfishness and the lack of sharing?

- Do you renounce the spirit of wanting more than you need?
- Do you renounce the spirit of evil that leads to judging others?
- Do you believe in the Spirit of God living in you?
- Do you believe that through Baptism we are called to be Christ to one another?

When you finish exploring the meaning of your baptismal promises, close your reflection with this prayer:

> Let us pray, then, for ourselves and for all those who will be baptized this Easter season:
>
> > God of all that is good, guide us as we live your gospel.
> > Be with all those to be baptized.
> > May the light of your life be always within them.
> > May your living water always refresh us all.
> > Amen.

As a further reminder of Baptism, invite all to dip a hand into the bowl of water on the table and sign themselves with the Sign of the Cross.

# The Fourth Week of Lent:
# Almsgiving

Lenten discipline tends to fall into three categories: prayer, fasting and almsgiving. We have already discussed prayer and fasting in this book. This is almsgiving week.

In today's economy, almsgiving as we usually understand it is not a pleasant thought. "How can I, in conscience, give any money away?" a parent asked me recently. "I hardly have enough to feed and clothe my own family." This is a common query among families today—perhaps because our concept of almsgiving is too narrow.

Alms, to most of us, is a monetary donation. The danger in this "charity-by-the-checkbook" mentality is an accompanying concept of "salvation-by-the-checkbook."

We Americans have a tendency to think that money can alleviate all pain. To be sure, giving money can be very helpful; it can raise our consciousness in terms of the poor. But our money needs to be shared with an understanding of the *need* with which our donation brings us into solidarity.

For example, your family Lenten fasting project

during the second week of Lent helped you and your children understand hunger in the world a little better. You made a conscious effort toward alleviating it through your sacrifice and money. In the same spirit, children can be encouraged to use their allowance money for someone else rather than spend it all on themselves. Teens could be invited to drink one less can of cola each day and donate the cost to Operation Rice Bowl. But the overriding question that needs to be asked about all of this is, "Does it make a lasting difference in our own life?"

Almsgiving should make a difference in the *life-style* of the almsgivers, not simply in their bank balance. Similarly, almsgiving which "skims off the top" and does not evoke a sense of real sacrifice is hardly even worth the thought. Real charity comes not from our excess but from our need. Remember, the poor widow gave more than all the rich who contributed to the treasury (see Mark 12:41-44).

In addition, almsgiving needs to be viewed more as sharing than as check-writing. While the donation of money to the needy is good, it is often a rather impersonal form of sacrifice. A more personal form of almsgiving can be seen through our efforts to share something of ourselves. Sharing of our comfort, our time, our privacy, of all that we assume is ours by right is often more difficult than sharing our money. It can also effect a more radical change in us—a real conversion which check-writing cannot match. For example:

- Share the world's energy:
    Turn down the heat and put on a sweater.
    Turn off radios and stereos that are providing only background music for you.
    Wash dishes by hand instead of using the dishwasher.

Turn off unneeded lights.

Instead of driving walk wherever you can one or more days this week.

- Share your own energy:

  Help someone in the family do their chores.

  Make a concerted effort not to use all your energy in your work. Share it with your family.

  Ask older children to play with their younger brothers and sisters, no matter how silly their games seem, or to read them a bedtime story once or twice this week.

  Share the spring cleaning without grumbling.

- Share the earth:

  Begin recycling all your glass, cans and paper. Take them to a recycling center in your community.

  Start a plant from a slip of one of your own, or plant some spring bulbs in individual pots. At Easter take them to someone in a nursing home or to someone in your neighborhood who needs cheering up.

  Wrap all gifts—from birthdays to Christmas—in the Sunday comics instead of commercial gift-wrap.

  Take a family walk to a local park or around a lake or along a river. Bring a large trash bag and pick up all the debris you find along the way.

- Share your time:

  Visit a nursing home, whether you know anyone there or not.

  Take time to listen to someone you don't enjoy.

  Take time to write to congressional representatives, senators, the president on behalf of programs to help the needy.

Attend a city commission, parish council, board of education, or League of Women Voters meeting—something that would be really out of character for you.

Spend some quality time with each of your children this week—just you and the child.

Volunteer to tutor the handicapped or read to the blind.

Spend at least one extra hour together as a family this week. Do something besides watching TV or your own individual "thing."

• Share yourself:

Babysit for a mother who doesn't get out very often—without pay.

Give a hug to someone in your family who seems to be having a bad day.

Smile more often to let others know you want them to share your happiness.

Get into an adopt-a-grandparent program and spend an hour or so a week being friends with someone who is lonely.

Adopt a family with which to share all kinds of things.

When you do your spring cleaning this year, distribute all the things you no longer need or use to those who can use them. Some of the giving should hurt!

Take in a runaway.

Take in someone's children so mom and dad can have a whole day to themselves.

The lists could go on and on. You can probably add to all of them yourselves. The point, of course, is not that each family tries to do all of the suggested sharing ideas. They are presented only as suggestions to help you broaden your understanding of almsgiving. You might keep the list for ideas throughout the year; sharing and almsgiving are not solely a Lenten activity. If we are to experience a difference in our life-style, Christian sharing must become a constant in our lives.

### Family Almsgiving Activity

Get a sheet of paper for each member of the family. On the paper, print the person's name and each of the sharing categories: ("Share the World's Energy," "Share Your Own Energy," "Share the Earth," "Share Your Time," "Share Yourself"). Be sure to leave space between each of the categories.

Sit down as a family and talk about these forms of sharing, using some of the examples given or your own examples. Then go through the categories one by one and decide what you as a family or as individuals can do to share with others during the remainder of Lent.

Some of the categories might suggest individual sharing projects to some family members, especially if you have older children who want to feel more autonomous. Allowing them to have a sharing project that is independent of the rest of the family is an excellent way to help them learn what it means to be Christian. Some of the categories might suggest sharing that is just right for the whole family; for example, recycling, spring cleaning, adopting a family. Let those be sharing activities that the family does together. When the decision is made, ask each person to write the activity (whether individual or family) under the related category on the papers.

You may not accomplish all of the projects in one week. In fact, you may not even want to try to do all of them in that concentrated a time. Let this project last through the rest of Lent.

Once a week, though, get together as a family to

talk about what you have done, as individuals or as a family, in the area of almsgiving or sharing. Summarize the activity and the results on the papers, pray a prayer of praise ("Glory be to the Father, and to the Son...") and rejoice that you were able to re-treat yourselves to the basics of Christian almsgiving.

Add one more challenge to this project. Don't stop after Lent. Continue this project all year, complete with the weekly family meetings to share yourselves and your Christian witness with one another.

# The Fifth Week of Lent:
# Springtime

It is no accident that the Church's liturgical year is arranged in such a way that Lent and springtime coincide. In many respects, Lent and springtime are nearly synonymous, both symbolically and in actual fact.

As human beings we experience the periodic need for renewal and revitalization. For most of us that need peaks around February or March (during Lent and early spring) and is in many ways precipitated by our natural surroundings.

We watch our house plants as their bright green fades and they sit dormant and near death for three months or more. We tire of looking out at leafless trees and brown lawns or dirty snow. We wonder if our bushes and trees will survive the winter; we even wonder if we will survive the death of nature around us.

Cabin fever sets in as we come down from the highlights of Christmas and Epiphany; we experience an inner anxiety and uneasiness. The great desire for new life sprouting begins to creep into our bones as nature goes through the annual struggle between warm and cold, sunshine and clouds, flowers and frost.

The Church in her wisdom responds to that natural season and to the needs each of us has by giving us the season of Lent at the time of spring. In fact, the practices of Lent are about as old as spring itself. The date of Easter Sunday is directly tied to the arrival of spring; it is always the first Sunday after the first full moon of spring. The Gospels all place the death and resurrection of Jesus at the time of Passover, celebrated the week of the first full moon of spring; the Last Supper was a celebration of the Passover meal.

Passover itself, though it commemorates the Exodus event, actually had pre-Exodus springtime origins. It was a spring agricultural festival celebrated by nomadic farmers long before the time of Moses and the Israelites' slavery in Egypt. After the Exodus of the Israelites, the agricultural festival acquired an added historical dimension: It celebrated not only life from the death of winter, but also life from the death of slavery. Springtime was the best natural metaphor for understanding what happened to the Israelites in the Exodus experience. Springtime is also the best way for us to comprehend what happens to each of us on our Lenten journey to spiritual renewal and return to the Lord.

Spring helps us to be conscious of the wonder of life emerging from death. Through spring we can see the deepest affirmation of God's care and love for us. We see it in the ways we die to our inner selfishness through our Lenten fasting and sharing. We see it in the ways that we are more awake to the Spirit of God within us as expressed through our Lenten prayer. We see it in remembering our Baptism, our celebration of death to sin and of new life in Christ. We see it in the Gospel for the Fifth Sunday of Lent (Cycle A) in the death and raising of Lazarus.

Our Christian faith sees in spring the meaning of our whole commitment to Jesus: a dying to selfishness, a dying to all the other "gods" that demand our allegiance in order to live in Christ, to live for others. We look at the seeds we plant in spring and see ourselves:

> "I tell you, most solemnly,
> unless a wheat grain falls on the ground and dies,
> it remains only a single grain;
> but if it dies,
> it yields a rich harvest."
> (John 12:24, *Jerusalem Bible*)

That death and rebirth does not happen overnight, any more than flowers and trees open into beautiful green and multicolored maturity after one spring rain. It takes time. Nature needs a number of warm days for buds to open and seeds to sprout. But eventually they do: Crocuses, tulips, jonquils, ferns and early wild flowers begin to poke their heads through the leftover snow. Ice on lakes and rivers eventually breaks, exposing dark blue water. Spring rains come to dispel the drought and dirtiness of winter and wash away the mud of many months.

We begin Lent much like nature begins Lent, weighted down with muddiness, as it were. We have need of the spring rains to soften our parched selfishness, to wash away the dust that has accumulated on our spiritual lives and re-treat us to the sproutings of new life that God holds out for us.

It is important that we be open to the workings of God all around us so that, with nature and with the farmer, we can plow under the dead deeds of winter and plant the new seeds of spring. The deeper we bury the dead deeds, the better is our "soil" prepared for new growth, new life.

**Family Springtime/New Life Activity**

Let your family activity this week be your response to the wonders and glories of resurrection that God reveals through nature.

Spend a significant amount of time outdoors with your family this week. Go for walks and observe the new growth. Look for blooming wild flowers. Pick some pussy willows, tulips or jonquils if they are blooming in your area. Add them to your prayer corner. Cut some lilac or forsythia branches, put them in water and watch them leaf out right before your eyes. Look closely at the buds of trees. Choose one tree on your street and go out to observe its new life each day.

If possible, plant something in your flower or vegetable garden this week, or start seedlings indoors. If you have a lake or river nearby, notice how blue the water is. Listen to the sound of a river or stream rushing with new life. If you live on a farm, new life is hatching and being born all around you. Let it speak to you. Look for the "resurrection" of creeping or flying creatures. Listen to the sounds of birds returning from warmer climates. Smell the clean freshness of the air. Touch the softness of life that is new.

Become keenly aware of the new life around you and the new life budding within you because of a Lent well lived. You, like nature, are undergoing the struggle that is spring. You are returning to the Lord who calls you to "come forth" to new life as he called to Lazarus.

One caution in your spring walks this week: Don't say anything to your children about all of this imagery. Just let them fill their senses with it all. Let them collect as many signs of spring and new life as they want—children love to collect things.

Then, on the Saturday before Passion (Palm) Sunday, sit down together. Gather whatever has been collected, and ask: "How has our family grown during this Lent? How are we like all the signs of spring we have seen this week?"

Re-treat yourselves to your own newness and be glad!

## The Climax of Lent:
# Holy Week

Only one week of the entire Church year is called "holy." It is so called because it commemorates the last holy days of Christ's life, his death and resurrection, but also because it calls us to holiness. This is the week that we are called to remember our Christian roots and our own life, death and resurrection. This is the week when we enact the words that we repeat each week when we "proclaim the mystery of our faith" in the Eucharistic Prayer: "Christ has died, Christ is risen, Christ will come again." This is the week we are called to the banquet, called to the service of each other, called to the cross, called to the joy of our return to God, called to the glory of the Resurrection and filled with new Christ-life, called to our own resurrectional reunion in heaven.

But Holy Week does not exist by itself. Everything that has happened during the weeks of Lent builds up to this week. Everything that has happened in our own re-treat to the basics of the mystery of suffering, death and resurrection in ourselves opens up and reveals itself to us this week. Lent is incomplete for us without the celebration of Holy Week.

The importance of ritualizing this mystery and reality of our faith cannot be emphasized too greatly. And so the best family activity that I can recommend to you this week is to *celebrate the liturgies of these holy days with your family in your parish.* They are so rich and so full of meaning that the liturgies themselves are sufficient for a family Holy Week experience.

The author Earnest Larson once said, however, "Liturgy begins at home," and I believe that. So, while I encourage you to go with your family to all of the liturgies of Holy Week, I also invite you to begin at home by spending some time each morning of the week explaining to your children what is commemorated on each of the special days of Holy Week: Passion Sunday, Holy Thursday, Good Friday, Holy Saturday, Easter Sunday.

## Passion Sunday

Holy Week begins with Passion Sunday, the day that we recall Jesus' truimphant journey into Jerusalem, where he was hailed as King and had palm branches and flowers strewn in his path. Over the years, the emphasis came to be placed on the palms, even to the point that the day's other name is Palm Sunday. The palms which we receive on this day, however, are a symbolic reminder of the real message of the day: We humans are fickle.

We are as fickle as the people of Jesus' time who one day proclaimed him king and a few days later hid in fear, denying that they ever heard of him. If we are willing to go to Jerusalem for the parade and the kingly proclamation, we had better realize what else waits for us there, and what is expected of us as Christians. It might be a good idea to restore an old Italian custom of exchanging palms with someone we may have offended during the year to remind us of our fickleness and to ritualize our conversion.

The liturgy of the day, if we observe carefully, speaks to us of that fickleness and need for conversion. It is a schizophrenic liturgy: First comes the story of that joyous entry into Jerusalem, with the blessing and distribution of palms—and often with our own reenactment of that glorious parade. Then the mood changes rather abruptly, as we are asked to hold those same palms and listen to the proclamation of the Passion, the prediction (or reminder) of what awaits us in Jerusalem.

Maybe it was to remind her of that reality that Grandma always came home from the Passion Sunday liturgy and put the new palm branch she received behind the crucifix.

## Holy Thursday

Holy Thursday marks the end of Lent. That's right—Thursday, not Friday or Saturday. With the evening Mass of the Lord's Supper the Church leaves Lent behind and begins the celebration of the death and resurrection of Christ. Holy Thursday, Good Friday and Easter together make one great feast, the *Triduum* ("three days"), the high holy days of the Christian calendar.

By the time Holy Thursday arrives, our family and parish Lenten retreat should have brought us to the point of reconciliation, of being once again in face-to-face peace with God and with one another. Those who wish should have availed themselves of the Sacrament of Reconciliation by this time, so that the liturgy of Holy Thursday can be a joyous celebration of our return at the banquet of the Lord. Indeed, many parishes do not even schedule confessions during the Triduum.

The liturgy of Holy Thursday is a celebration of the Lord's Supper and all that implies. At the table of the Lord we break open the Word for one another, we break bread for one another; and in that action we express our willingness to serve and minister to one another.

The Washing of the Feet is told in the Gospel and sometimes reenacted during the liturgy. Jesus' command (*mandatum*) to imitate his action gives this day its name, Maundy Thursday, as a further expression of what Eucharist is all about. Eucharist is more than sharing the Body and Blood of Jesus with one another. It is also sharing all that Jesus is for us—and that is best expressed in the way we serve and minister to one another, as Jesus did in his lifetime.

### Good Friday

A few years ago, I received an early Good Friday morning call from a parent who was explaining the meaning of Good Friday to her children. Seven-year-old David, who had listened attentively to the whole explanation, finally asked: "So what's so good about Good Friday? It seems like it should be called Bad Friday."

True, Good Friday is a day to reflect on Jesus' crucifixion and death. In and of itself, there's not much good in that. But Good Friday is also a day to recall that because of Jesus' great giving of self, we can live and have the assurance of eternal life.

The liturgy of the day does this well with the proclamation of the Passion, prayers for the Church and the world, and veneration of the cross as the banner of victory of life over death. No Mass is celebrated, but we receive Communion as a sign that Jesus' death nourishes our life. And that's what's so good about Good Friday. If there had been no Good Friday, there would be no Easter—for Jesus or for us!

### The Easter Vigil

Sometime between sunset on Holy Saturday and sunrise on Easter morning, the Church celebrates the resurrection of Jesus in the service that is the high point of the liturgical year: the Easter Vigil. It begins with waiting in the darkness that fell over the earth Good Friday afternoon—a darkness that is shattered by the lighting of the Easter fire and the Easter candle, the light of the risen Lord.

The new light spreads throughout the darkened church as believers light individual candles from the Easter candle, and the Easter Proclamation (the *Exultet*) calls them to joy with triumphant song:

> Rejoice, heavenly powers! Sing, choirs of angels!
> > Exult, all creation around God's throne!
> > Jesus Christ, our King, is risen!
> > Sound the trumpet of salvation!
> Rejoice, O earth, in shining splendor,
> > radiant in the brightness of your King!

A lengthy series of Scripture readings tells the story of salvation history, the story of God's dealings with our world since the beginning of creation. Then the water of the baptismal font is blessed, and the catechumens come forth for the sacrament they have so long prepared to receive. (In the early Church, the Vigil was the *only* celebration of Baptism.) For the rest of us, too, it is a celebration of our entry into the new life Christ has won for us as we repeat our own baptismal vows. Finally, all the baptized share the Eucharist.

The Easter Vigil is a rather long service for children but, with ample preparation, can be a marvelous learning and worship experience for them since it is a dramatic and symbolically rich service. To be able to appreciate it, children should first of all be somewhat familiar with the story of the history of our salvation, especially the story of creation, the story of the Israelites' freedom from slavery, and the story of our own liberation from sin to salvation through the life, death and resurrection of Jesus.

They should be helped to understand that the lighting of the great Easter fire is a symbol of Christ, the Light of the World who triumphed over the darkness of evil. The lighted Easter (Paschal) candle is the lasting symbol in our church of Christ risen. It stands throughout the Easter season until Pentecost as a reminder to us of the risen Lord's presence; it is lit for all Baptisms and funerals throughout the year as a reminder of our own resurrection.

The Baptism of adult catechumens can be more meaningful if children have been told of the story of their own Baptism (see pages 24-26). Joining in the renewal of baptismal promises can be the beginning of their own acceptance of the faith. It also enables them to experience being a part of a supportive, welcoming community.

## Easter Sunday

The Lord is risen, alleluia! This day of great joy is filled with symbols of resurrection and new life. Following are some of those symbols and customs which are very much a part of Easter Sunday and the Easter season. Many of them we tend to simply take for granted. Share them with your children to help them understand the significance of some of our Easter customs and some of the symbolism of this beautiful season of resurrection and new life.

*Easter Lilies.* The Easter lily has acquired a religious symbolism and quite appropriately so. Its radiant whiteness, the delicate beauty of its bugle-shaped form make it an eloquent herald of the Easter celebration. It is mentioned often in the Scriptures as a symbol of beauty, perfection and goodness.

The Easter lily is larger than the more generally

known Madonna lily. It was introduced in Bermuda (from Japan) at the middle of the last century. In 1882 the florist W.K. Harris brought it to the United States and spread its use here. Since it flowers first around Eastertime in this part of the world, it soon came to be called the Easter lily. The American public immediately accepted it and made it a symbolic feature of the Easter decorations in their homes and churches.

*Easter Eggs.* In ancient times eggs were a symbol of spring and fertility. An egg seems dead and yet contains new life. This is the reason why people in pre-Christian ages presented each other with eggs at the beginning of spring.

In medieval times the eating of eggs was prohibited during Lent, so Christians transferred the custom of giving eggs to Easter Sunday. Instead of representing fertility, the Easter egg now became a symbol of the rock tomb out of which our Lord gloriously emerged to new life. The Church even has a ritual blessing for eggs.

Perhaps you would like to pray this simple blessing over your decorated Easter eggs this week:

> *All extend their hands over the eggs as one member of the family prays the blessing:*

> We praise you, O God, for these signs of life, our Easter eggs.
> We thank you for the bright, bursting forth of Christ our Lord.
> Amen! Alleluia!

*The Easter Bunny.* Hares and rabbits served our pre-Christian ancestors as symbols of fertility because they multiply so fast. They were kept in homes and given as presents at the beginning of spring. From this ancient custom the story of the Easter Bunny developed in

Germany in the 15th century. Little children delight in the traditional fairy tale that Easter eggs are produced and brought by the Easter bunny.

*Easter Clothes.* The tradition of wearing new clothes on Easter Sunday is practiced by many of us in this country, and appropriately so. This custom goes back to the early centuries of Christianity.

The early Christians, most of whom were baptized as adults, used to wear the white gowns they were given at their Baptism throughout the whole Easter week as a symbol of their new life. The other Christians, who had already been baptized, did not wear white garments, but they dressed in new clothes at Easter to indicate that they, too, had risen to new life in Christ. All believers have put off the old way and put on Jesus' way. The wearing of new clothes at Easter is an external profession, a symbol of the Easter grace: spiritual resurrection to a better and holier life.

*Easter Water.* In the liturgy of Holy Saturday night, the presiding priest solemnly blesses the Easter water, which will be used during the service for Baptism. An appropriate activity for your family can be to take home a small container of this Easter water to be used during the Easter season for family blessings of persons, the house, even the Easter dinner. Each blessing can serve as a reminder of the new life which we celebrate at this time of year.

*Easter Pastry.* Most families of European descent have a traditional Easter bread, a custom received from their ancestors: Russian *Paska,* German *Osterstollen,* Polish *Baba Wielanocna,* etc. Very often these breads and pastries, together with meat and eggs, were blessed by the parish priest on Holy Saturday.

An Italian custom is to make a simple sweet bread dough shaped in the form of a chick, bunny or doll. These breads are baked with a whole egg placed in the "tummy" of the form and glazed with egg yolk. They are given as gifts on Easter Sunday to young friends and relatives.

*Easter Parade.* Our modern Easter parades originated during the Middle Ages as a religious custom which is still kept in its ancient form in some sections of Central Europe. Dressed in their new clothes, the people take the so-called "Easter Walk" after Easter Sunday Mass. They march in a well-ordered column through the town and into the countryside. A crucifix decorated with flowers or the Easter candle leads the procession. While walking the people pray or sing Easter hymns.

After the Reformation this traditional Easter walk lost its religious significance in some countries and was continued only as a popular custom. It came to this country from England and developed into the famous Easter parade held annually in our big cities on Easter Sunday.

Whether you march in an Easter parade or not, may Easter be for you and your family a truly joyous and holy season. May the New Life begun in your family this Lent express itself as you continue to be alleluia people all year long.

# Beyond Lent:
# The Easter Season

Don't stop now. You've only just begun. Lent is not a self-contained season, isolated in and of itself. The goal of Lent is Easter. From start to finish, Lent is a preparation for Easter. And Easter is not just a day, it is a *season* that lasts for 50 days. So keep celebrating and re-treating yourselves to the presence of the risen Lord.

- Have an Emmaus Day. Luke's Gospel (24:13-35) tells the story of two disciples on the road from Jerusalem to Emmaus on the day of the Resurrection. They meet a stranger on the way, whom they finally recognize as the Lord when he breaks bread with them. On the Sunday after Easter, go someplace the family has always wanted to go and see how often you meet and recognize the risen Lord on the way. Remember, sometimes he can be found in symbols of new life as well as in people.
- Have a picnic breakfast some Saturday or Sunday morning during the Easter Season, like Jesus and the apostles did on the shores of the Sea of

Tiberias (see John 21:1-12).
- The feast of the Ascension is the 40th day after Easter. Get some balloons, put special messages of joy inside them and let them ascend into the air. Who knows, when they land they may help someone else's spirits be raised!
- Do you plant a garden? How about giving those seeds a special blessing before or after they're planted? If your family brought holy water home from the Easter Vigil service, use some of it for this purpose.
- The 50th day of Easter is Pentecost. Go fly a kite, take a ride in a swing, breathe deeply, inhale, exhale, gasp, whistle, wheeze, chase the wind, or just let the wind blow in your face. On the first Pentecost the folks in the Upper Room heard a wind, took a deep breath and felt the presence of God around and within them (see Acts 2:1-4).

May you, too, feel that wonderful closeness of God in your family. May this little book help you to re-treat yourselves to the gift of new life that is Lent and Easter. And may the presence of God that you find in that newness of life remain with you and yours always.